AGESONG

Meditations for Our Later Years

ELIZABETH BUGENTAL

Elders Academy Press

AgeSong: Meditations for Our Later Years is sponsored and published by Elders Academy Press, a program of Pacific Institute. Pacific Institute teaches new perspectives on aging in the field of gerontology and aims to reestablish the role of eldership in our society. The Institute is a nonprofit educational corporation that promotes individual and community wellness and helps advance, disseminate, and preserve knowledge in gerontological fields that focus on clinical, educational and human services purposes. *www.pacificinstitute.org*

Elders Academy Press seeks to help change perceptions of the elderly and aging and develop a vision of a contemporary Elder. The Press also seeks to encourage people to approach the process of aging with consciousness and to direct their thoughts toward to possibilities ahead.

Elders Academy Press
432 Ivy Street
San Francisco, California 94102
www.elderspress.org

First Edition

Printed in the United States

Jacket Design Emily Tanner, The Knitting Brigade, *www.theknittingbrigade.com*
Interior Design Emily Tanner and Piotr Orlik

Elders Academy Press' publications are available through most bookstores. For further information, call 415-861-3455 or visit our website at *www.elderspress.org*. Substantial discounts on bulk quantities are available to corporations, professional associations, and other organizations. Email info@elderspress.org for details and discount information.

Library of Congress Cataloging-in-Publication Data
Bugental, Elizabeth
 Agesong : meditations for our later years/Elizabeth Bugental.--1st
ed.
  p. cm.
 ISBN 0-9758744-4-6
1. Older people--Poetry. 2. Aging--Poetry. 3. Older people. 4.
Aging. I. Title.
 PS3602.U355A34 2004
 811'.6--dc22

For all the beauty and goodness that surrounds me and keeps my life rich, especially Jim.

PUBLISHER'S NOTE

This is a rare book. Like life itself, it took time to birth it, make it public. From the first moment of reading Elizabeth Bugental's manuscript—now almost ten years ago—until today, her writing has stayed with me. Whereas Elizabeth showed no interest in making her work available to anyone but who would specifically ask for it, I began excerpting her manuscript in hand-outs, newsletters and books. Everywhere readers were taken by the depth and wisdom of her writing. A few years ago we established Elders Academy Press with the mission to promote books intent on changing the dominant perceptions of aging. Her manuscript now belongs to the first books pulished under this venture. We feel honored to bring Elizabeth's remarkable poems to you.

Nader R. Shabahangi
Elders Academy Press

MEDITATIONS

INTRODUCTION

This morning my husband and I had a conversation at the breakfast table. It began when he looked up from the paper to ask me how old he was, and progressed from there to all kinds of other questions about his life. I conjured up some memories for him, images and vignettes—his adult children, our daughter and her husband, our family and friends, his achievements, books he had written, wonderful celebrations in his honor, special moments between us, our travels—until it became clear that he was listening avidly to a tale about someone he didn't even know. I reached across the table to hold his hand as the tears ran down his cheeks, explaining to him, as I have many many times, that a stroke a year and a half ago had simply wiped out his past. He was quiet for awhile, bathed in grief. Then he looked up, the tears still standing in his eyes. "But I have you," he said, smiling. He sat a minute, struggled to his feet, dragging himself slowly on his walker into the living room and his favorite chair facing out the window into the garden.

When I came in a few minutes later and stood behind him looking out, my arms around his neck, he covered my hands with his. "I am out there naked in the sun and the wind," he said. "We have such a good life."

Almost everything I want to say in this book is here, in this everyday story. We live our lives and, if we're lucky or maybe smart, or both, we do mostly what we meant to do. Then it ends. Perhaps very slowly, like Jim's. If we're fortunate enough to participate in the aging process we have time to prepare ourselves, as our bodies, and perhaps our minds, run down. With conscious choices and an ability to stay in the moment, we might even bring joy and quiet pleasure to this final life phase. Possibly, even excitement.

When I first wrote *AgeSong*, over ten years ago, a dear younger friend was dying of cancer. As I wrote, I lamented, "Mondi will never get to live this part of her life," and because she was someone who did everything with zest and enthusiasm, I grieved for her loss as I grieved the loss of her in my life. This last stage of life is a precious gift as is every other stage. We mourn the death of a child or a young person, feeling it an aberration. He or she will never get to experience all the lively, passionate moments of their maturing years including the slow, lingering ticking away of these winding-down days.

I wrote these words out of my own need to be a participant in what was happening to me anyway in these later years. I wanted to ascend in my declining, to notice and learn and enjoy and savor, as I had in my teens and twenties and my middle years. I couldn't imagine simply falling out of life like the leaves from the trees as my body gave out. If I could bring it off, I wanted to fly. But I had to discover where the wings were and find the place inside that would propel me. I knew there were storms ahead over which I had no control, but whatever the weather, I wanted to do everything I could to stay quietly, even passionately, afloat in the moment, to taste the life still available in the letting go.

I do not disavow my blueprint now, and in some ways it has been put to the test. I re-read my own words as a reminder. But I am not, I hope, naïve or blasé. Living long takes its toll. Our skin is fragile. We bruise easily. No matter how we prepare for the sting, we jump when the needle touches the skin. Physical and mental pain are real and can be all-encompassing. I leave that to better people than I to describe and prescribe.

Even so, these final years are a privilege. Children starve in Sudan, youngsters die in Iraq. We are here to bear a kind of witness only age can provide, even as the sadness of loss dims our sight. We are allowed to walk slowly and reverently among the debris, picking up whatever we can save, mourning what we cannot. One by one we lose our life-long companions. The generation before us, consolers and counselors, has left us to clean up what we can. Crises are a way of life. And yet, if given a choice, most of us would embrace the chance to walk that last slow victory lap around the arena of our lives, wrapped in the banner of our years, scattering along the way whatever small wisdom, comfort, and appreciation we may have to offer.

I'm learning still, writing the *Final Chorus* of the song of age. I'm observing as I'm living, hoping I can stay just ahead or, at least, alongside the rush of years overtaking me. I am filled with gratitude for the feeling and the pace of this last lap with my husband, eleven years ahead of me on the course. It is, quite simply, an undeserved grace, lavishly bestowed. At the very end I will run out of words. No matter, I'll be somewhere else, beyond the shabby gesture of language.

Elizabeth Bugental

AgeSong

HOW DID I GET TO BE THIS OLD?

Old was never. Faded gray like fog.
Somebody else walking too slowly, blocking the path.
    Brush past.
    Look away quickly.
    Forget quickly. Look ahead.
    Misshapen toes in old slippers aren't fun.

Coming closer now. Can't say it looks much better
from the outside. Like our young adult children heading
for foreign countries, trying to imagine new lives,
we're dealing with millions of unknowns.

That's strange.
What did we think these later years would be like?
Or did we think at all about life
after ever-lengthening *middle age?*

Oh, there were lots of *afters*.
    After the kids leave home.
    After we quit work.
    After the house sells.
    After his back surgery.
    After her hysterectomy.
    After mom's settled in the retirement home.
    After our money's invested safely.

Long list of *afters*.

But we didn't anticipate much about our insides.
>   Didn't know we'd still be noticing swaggering
>   guys in tight jeans.
>   Bright red lipstick on young girls.
>   Green leaves pushing out of dead-looking twigs.

Didn't know that giving up on *knowing it all*
might leave us feeling smarter than ever.
Didn't know we'd like ourselves in new ways.
Didn't know we'd be unable to keep our feet quiet when
the music starts.
Didn't know we'd still be looking for answers.
Feel even more invested in our world.
Care so much about
>   kids
>   clean air
>   disappearing species
>   struggling single mothers
>   street violence
>   the Middle East

Didn't know we'd still be crying at the movies.
>   Trying to define religion.
>   Locate the Deity.
>   Document an afterlife.

Didn't know we'd still be wondering about death.

Didn't know we could still be
 diminished by jealousy
 reduced by rage
 wearied by childhood demons

Didn't know we'd feel so good, even contented.
 Like waking up in the morning, planning our day.
 Feel more passionate than ever about family
 and friends.
 Be thrilled at births and weddings, desolate
 at funerals.
 Didn't know that life could get more precious
 rather than less.

Well, we each have our own personal lists.
Particulars vary.
What surprises you about being this age?

Yes, it's not over yet, is it?
We're extra careful crossing busy streets, driving
on freeways. We read the soup can labels, toss out
old medicines. Jog around the malls, do aerobics.
Spread out the annuity, worry over health insurance.
Yeah, counting on at least twenty more years.
Older's much younger than we thought.

SAYING THE NEVERS

Still ...
We'll never be young again.

That's a hard word: *never*.
"Never say *never*."
Wrong.
Need to say it now. Selectively, of course.
     I'll never be young again.
     I'll never have that perfect body.
     I'll never know all there is to know.
     I'll never do all I meant to do.
     I'll never see all I wanted to see.
     I'll never be as noble as I hoped to be.
     I'll never be famous.
     I'll never be first.
     I'll never be a hero.
     I'll never see my grandchildren grow old.
     Never ... never ... never ... never.

Yes, say them all.

Because *someday*
     and *maybe*
     and *perhaps*
     keep us dangling over into tomorrows

using up our time
taking up precious space.

Pining over yesterday.
Longing for another chance at youth.
Pretending away the years.
Wastes whatever we have left to spend.

Never sweeps clean.
Never leaves room for something else.

"I'll never be young again" means we get to be older,
even *old*. We've never done that before.
It's a new adventure.
"No," says the youngster inside us.
"Try it out," says the adventurer, always ready
for a different experience.

CREATING AN OLD AGE

If we use our own muscles we can shape our old age.
Whereas if we only let the years happen to us,
we're just dragged along ...
    passive
    inert
    voiceless
No adventure in that.

I'll never be young again.

There, that's not so hard.
We're getting better with practice.

So how long's this *older-old* going to last?
    Ten years?
    Twenty?
    Thirty?
    Who knows?
Who reads the life-expectancy charts?
We do.
Amortize the pension. Again.
Recount the bonus years.
And what's this *old* stuff?
The question's a little unmanageable.
Like winding spaghetti on a fork,

trying to get a decently polite mouthful.
I can't quite get to the end of it.
That's OK. I always did have a big mouth.

Twenty or more years, huh?
How to live it?
How to even think about it?

So many unknowns...
Yeah, but there always were.
Think of the unexpected twists and turns
your younger life took when you weren't looking.

WHAT'S DIFFERENT NOW?

Now we're a bit more wary
Feel a bit more vulnerable.
Our bodies don't quite hold up as they once did.
We get tired more easily, don't bounce back as fast.
Our earning power's decreased
And et cetera.

On the other hand, there are some unexpected freedoms.
When we were younger, we had to be focused, carefully
placing one foot in front of the other, climbing
the determination ladder to get where we are now,
rung after rung of plans and ambitions.
As the saying goes, we did what we had to do.

It's different now.

Work

The meaning of work shifted sometime recently.
The ladder leading up and up straightened out
onto solid ground. The grass can now grow quietly
and safely under our feet.

Though some of us still have jobs, most of us don't
define ourselves by them as we once did.

We're not blind. Glancing over our shoulders,
we notice our successors hovering impatiently
in the background. Though some economic necessity
may still poke and prod us into action,
we've outgrown the grabbing and getting
for possessions or promotions. For many of us
with some financial security, work means something
new, more pure, more for itself, as in *my work*,
more personal somehow.

She might want to paint cabbages,
answer phones on a hot line. He might
design kites, carve wooden squirrels,
push wheelchairs in a hospital,
write poetry.
I might like sitting on a park bench or on the beach
staring at the seagulls, doing nothing at all.

Janet, at 14, wanted to be an ice-skater and a dancer.
She worked hard and accomplished both. In her thirties
she returned to school, became a teacher,
even authored a textbook. Now, in her sixties, retired,
she's ready to do something new. But she says
she wants to do it differently this time, without
so much rush. She's not even sure what she means
by this, but she's allowing herself to move
very, very slowly.

John says he doesn't believe in old age.
Brought up in near poverty,
he won a scholarship to Stanford,
started a business, became successful
beyond his dreams. He loves going to work
and shows up every day.
But at 68, he tells me he's moved his office to the back
of the building, delegates more, encourages
his employees to take more initiative. He's writing
a journal of his observations and feelings about
everything from his grandchildren to world affairs,
considers himself a savvy old consultant
to the business he once ran with an iron hand.

Fran, always a nature lover, her children raised,
her professional life as a physician over,
volunteers hours every week for the Audubon Society,
conducts science projects for kids.

Jim, a successful psychologist, author, and lecturer,
stopped seeing patients at 72. He writes and teaches
more than ever, but finds it easier, more natural,
more spontaneous and deeply satisfying.
Younger therapists instinctively value his genuineness,
honesty, willingness to share his foibles as well as his
triumphs. "I never could have trusted myself this much
when I was younger," he says.

Sally, the clothes freak, runs a thrift shop
for her church.

Dorothy, the avid reader, edits books for a small
publishing company.

Going to work changes meaning as we age.
We soon discover, after regular work hours disappear,
that our time fills anyhow. Time passes, even if
we stay indoors all day with the doors
and windows shut.

Money makes a difference too.
But whether we have a lot or a little, we know
a bit more about matching our incomes to our
occupations. After all, we've come through
depressions, inflations, unemployment,
and bank failures. We've been around.

We know if we want to we can do better at living
simply in order to simply live. If we can avoid stress,
we'll be more able to stretch out a hand to those
in real poverty who don't have as many choices.

Avoid the stress.
Is less stress really possible these days? Perhaps.
If we're willing to trade for a no-frills kind of life.

Libraries, parks, small vegetable gardens,
lots of walking. Church, community meetings,
senior centers, television, newspapers, books,
recorded music. All pretty cheap.
Not too bad.

Status

Some people never lose their love of the limelight.
My friend, Tom, after years of teaching school,
is becoming an actor, with lessons, glossies,
and demo tapes to prove it.

Well, why not, if it works?
Do we have the will,
the abilities, the high energy
to offset fading youth and beauty?

That's one way to age, dancing in the spotlight
till the final curtain.
But most of us probably lack that drive, or aren't
that clever. No one pays us a lot of attention
anymore. Our children, our students, our trainees
replace us front and center.
At the family picnic, the dinner table, or the company
reunion, we're watching from the sidelines. From the
wings, we're pushing our successors into the light.

Their turn to find themselves, decide on a career,
a vocation, make a place in the sun.
Thank goodness!
We don't have to prove ourselves.
We don't?
Are you sure?

Well, maybe we still do, but not for the same reasons.
Who, outside ourselves, cares anymore?
As my niece said,
"Okay, we know you can cook a good meal.
Don't knock yourself out for us."

There's nobody out there needing us to succeed.
Who cares anymore? Not mom or dad or our favorite
teachers. Our kids, our friends tell us (only faintly
interested), "Whatever you want." They might
even mean it.

This is getting scary!

Looks

An older woman's walking down the street ahead
of me. I know she's older, in spite of the tight skirt,
the spike heels, the flamboyantly dyed hair. As I move
up beside her I want to stare at the thickly painted

face, the tightly buttressed body. My immediate
amusement turns to sadness. Her disguise isn't
working. Her screaming defiance at the years only
calls attention to them.

I might inwardly salute such grim determination
to defy age. But, more likely, identifying with her,
I'm embarrassed at her self-delusion.

Each morning as I greet my own aging face
in the mirror with some astonishment,
I wonder, as I imagine she does,
how much to let be, how much to disguise.
I'm more like her than different.
She's just opted for the extreme end
of the spectrum.

Developing a whole new way of looking at ourselves
isn't an easy shift in an image-conscious world.
Yet, it could be a great relief. What if we really believed
didn't have to be magazine-beautiful?
The ads say, "Free yourself, get rid of the gray!"
They should say, "Gray hair frees."
No need to be cute and sexy, muscular and macho,
to compare and feel
            too fat
            too thin

too flat
too lumpy

Welcome to *attractive older*.

Oh, yeah?

Okay. So you caught yourself dipping into *Vogue*,
imbibing *Glamour*, sneaking a peek at *Playboy*.

Those young girls and boys inside our bodies stir,
respond, strut, and preen, tend to forget the years.

Well, all right …
A small regret here. A recurrent obsession with fashion.
Some yearning sighs for whistles, turning heads,
for second glances,
the wandering eyes … and hands.

But there! It goes. Yes, we're catching on to that.
Hold on to trying for a bit, till the job's too big,
too time consuming, a bore.

Youth-mourning could last a lifetime.

And hey! That *never look young again* cleared some
unexpected new space. Squint. Shut your eyes,

and open them again. Let go of that critical
appraising eye that only saw
what wasn't *model-perfect*: bones, bulge, and blemish

Now look again.
We're more free to see.
We can rejoice anew in color, fabric, style, ornament,
grace, form. These still remain.

We can play around.
Try on.
Enjoy a more personal costuming. Please ourselves.
How about it?
Can we breathe easier now?
Can we learn to mirror-gaze with different eyes?

Can we accept this older person looking back,
requiring so much less?
Can we play a little now, outfitting and draping
these old bones and flesh?

We have some help ... oh, yes.

Give one small cheer for merciful nearsightedness—our
new myopia-enlarged vision.
It allows us to enjoy what remains
when the hard edges disappear.

Competition

I'd like to be rid of the habit of comparing myself
to others, sizing up and measuring, coming out
on the top or the bottom.

The reality of age should have asserted itself
by now. I can't even hope to be the best-looking,
the smartest, the most powerful, certainly not
the youngest. No matter who I am, somebody younger,
perhaps even brighter, is looking me over, waiting
for a chance to grab my chair.

Sometimes I feel as if the alternative to competing
is to fade into the wallpaper, curl like a cat in the corner
waiting for an eye to light on me, a kindly hand
offering a friendly pat.

Then I remember the rules are different now.
Although I may be young, scintillating, full of ideas
under my skin, that's not what's visible anymore
(except perhaps by old friends who remember when).
If I'm still caught in the competition game, I lose.
But since I've become less of a threat, my power
as an intermediary, a facilitator, has increased.
Thoughtful listeners are rare. Age and benevolence
turn out to be natural partners.

I'll have to practice moving inside myself
when the old games seduce. At this stage of life,
winning isn't what it used to be. That's a comfort.
We don't have to win in the old way anymore.

Not a contest ... or a race ...
Not a battle or a tug-o-war for heart or hand.
What you see is what you get or don't get,
Want or don't want, love or don't.

Combat's no longer needed.
Except, perhaps, for extra spice, a little juice.

In our better moments we understand this ...
We know that buying and selling of goods
or affections is a game. Fun, perhaps,
or heartbreaking, but an illusion.
We never have total control of the playing field.

We've always been receivers, even when
we thought we had the ball all to ourselves.
Somebody else threw it, shoved it in our face,
or fumbled.

They've always been out there, those others
who accepted or rejected us. But, rushing on our way,
we simply pretended to be in charge, manipulating *them*

into admiration or love. We thought
we were doing it all. Every once in awhile
we'd put out our best effort and still lose.
What a shock!
What went wrong?

Now we know we never had all that power.
We're only really in charge
when we're giving stuff away.
And, even then, if we've attached a lot of strings,
we're liable to fall flat when they're broken.

It's the *giver* who really decides it all:
    who gets the gift
    when to give it
    and how
We know that now. And we can still be givers.

So here we stand just as we are, appreciating
whatever attention comes our way,
Trying to give back a bit more honestly,
Fooling nobody anyhow.
A new kind of winning.

WHO AM I (AGAIN)?

Coming back to the mirror ...

Who do I see now?

Who now?
>   If I don't have to be somebody special.

Who now?
>   If trying's not the game,
>   winning's not the goal,
>   attention's not the purpose?

Who now?
>   If riches aren't the reason,
>   possessions weigh beyond their worth,
>   pile up in storage, labeled,
>   marked for inheritance.

Who now?
>   If *Arriving*'s been and gone,
>   tomorrow an unexpected,
>   doubly-welcomed gift.

Who now?
>   If no one else is asking, only me?

Blankness.
Questions too hard to answer.

Change the subject. Think about something else.
Get busy.
There's always something to clean, file, polish,
remove, rearrange.
Get busy.

No. Stay. Let the emptiness enter.
Transition, it's called these days. *Transition*.
Means
>   wait
>   allow
>   trust
>   be still
An inner argument erupts.

"But that's a waste of time. So much yet to do."

"Yes, yes, so let's choose our busyness with care.
Make peace with who we are."

"Who I am?"

"Yes, but who you are is still in process. As long as
you're alive, no matter how old, your self-image blurs,

alters, enlarges every moment, continues to move ahead
just out of sight."

"But I wanted to arrive somewhere … be settled in
for once and all."

"In a way you are. But you'll have to face it,
just like your cells keep changing,
your mind and spirit change, multiply,
regroup, re-form."

"Well, I guess that's not so bad,
better than getting stuck or feeling disheartened
that I'll never be the ideal me.
But don't tell me I'm still changing.
I never did buy into all that *Who am I?* stuff.
Do I really need reminding who I am
and what I've done,
as if I've mislaid my memory?"

"Well, maybe not, but isn't it hard to feel
really connected to all that past history?"

"I'm beginning to get what you're saying.
Who is that youngster in the photograph
standing beside that ancient automobile?
Not *I* surely."

About Looking Back

These days, when I meet somebody new whom
I'd really like to know, I'm torn about whether
to make the effort. I wish there were a way
to implant our histories into each other's heads.
      Where to start?
      What to tell?
      What to leave out?
Should we just not bother at all with the past?

When I do finally begin to sketch out my story,
I'm often distracted by what I'm not saying,
the gaps in the narrative. I feel phony somehow,
or disappointed in the way the words are coming out,
almost as if I'm lying. There's so much ...
too much.

Talking about the past's like telling tales about
an insubstantial hero(ine) who keeps changing form.

At one moment she or he seems silly, vague,
incompetent, embarrassing really.

At another time ...
Look, mom! It's a super-achiever, dependability
personified, collector of letters and titles.

Neither and both hold the vital narrative.
Ho-hum. An oxymoron identity:
    the impersonal *true confession*.
    The anonymous obituary.
So who then?

Perhaps making lists would help.
    At ten I was …
    At twenty I did …
    At thirty … and so forth …
    Then I could read it like an index to a book.

"Would I believe it then? Would it tell me something
helpful—who to be now?"

"Well, maybe it's a start."

Elders are gathering in senior centers, writing journals,
drawing pictures, searching for something solid
to stand on, point to, show and tell somebody else.

Who am I, anyway?
The *Table of Contents* expands:
    fought in a war, did I?
    Had some babies, did I?
    What's left of all that?
We tell each other about ourselves.

"Yes, I once … "
"I used to be … "
"My son went to … "
I rode, walked, swam, built, sang, saw, worked,
loved, taught, received, gave, forgot.

Fill in the blanks. Create a life.
Yours. Mine. His. Hers. Our listeners
are polite, look mildly interested,
try to appear supportive.

Is that it? Do we have a *My Life* captured then?
If so, why don't we feel more substantial
in the collecting and the telling?

Perhaps because it's gone, at least that way
of grabbing a life won't work. It only makes
an awkward gesture backward.

We reach out to snatch time by the shoulders,
end up with a ragged piece of cloth clutched
in our fingers. We examine it over and over
for fingerprints, clues caught in the threads.
But it dematerializes in our hands.
Our litany of *when*'s, *how*'s, *where*'s ends up
looking like a torn and useless map to a place
that no longer exists.

So, who now?
Let's think about it another way …

I come upon a familiar bundle in a dark corner
of my closet.
If I hadn't been house cleaning I wouldn't have
discovered it.
When I untangle it I find old clothes, so familiar
I can't deny they're mine. They smell like me.

I've made this outfit over the years, woven it
from lived minutes. Then hidden it way in the back,
not liking the way it turned out. Or maybe just
thinking it belonged to someone else a little less
accomplished, less finished, less important,
less handsome.

So when I try on these old clothes,
a bit reluctantly, and look in the mirror,
the person looking back is strange,
not the one I expected (although if you asked me
what–who I expected, I couldn't have told you).

Certainly someone
    older
    wiser
    more complete

But what am I to do? There I am.

Wait. I recognize the smell, the tastes, sights,
touches flooding over. Mine. All mine.
The *memory-combinations* only I can remember.
My own *experiential puzzle* no one else
could put together quite the same.

What pops up on your memory screen?
What pictures appear? What feelings surface?

If anything lives after senses go, look here.
Forget the rest.

What can I do about the past?
Shut the closet behind me. Firmly.
It's full of old junk anyhow.
Did I really think I needed to hold on to it all?

Or could get rid of it? What really matters remains,
is firmly embedded in who I am today.
Just let the past be past.

Smile at the image in the mirror. Trust the reflection
looking back, today. Pull the costume round me.
Finger the texture, the multi-colored pains
        mistakes

> triumphs
> tragedies
> delights

Mine, all mine.
Get on with whatever's next.

Maybe I'll meet a wise older person I'd never
recognize in these old clothes. But, whether I do
or not, *I'll never get to repeat the past.*

WHAT'S NOW, WHAT'S AHEAD?

An ordinary phone conversation with my friend
Catherine carries a jolt of adrenalin without
the bad after-effects.

Catherine's a sort of genius at finding new
fascinations, projects, enthusiasms.

These past ten years, after leaving college teaching,
her pursuits have included yoga, ballroom dancing,
finance, folk singing, Swedish and oriental massage,
nutrition and painting. Even more importantly,
she's constantly reading, meditating, renewing
her inner resources, coming up with fresh insights.

What I'm admiring here isn't the variety
or number of her interests, but the intense level
of her involvement and pleasure. While most of us
are marching around the smorgasbord, waiting
for our taste buds to respond, she's relishing
the food that exactly satisfies her hunger.

Several times every year Catherine spends a week
alone, checking in with herself, distinguishing
her genuine wants and needs from the merely
expected or habitual. She tells me she gleans strength

and clarity in the solitude and silence, and returns
home to create the next few months
of her life in accordance with her deeper wishes.

Most of us haven't learned to do this very well.
After years of going along with the program, we're
out of touch with our deeper selves. Until we
unexpectedly burst into tears, have a temper
tantrum, realize we're sleeping too much, drowning
ourselves in television, tranquilizers, or alcohol,
we hardly recognize we're in trouble.

So how do we start to see again, create this later
life-phase using the wiser person inside us whom we
often forget to consult?

Wipe the Mirror Clean

Get a new vision. Yes.
Here we stand in our old accumulated outfits,
at the same time ridding ourselves of useless price tags
and trademarks, the outworn symbols
of an external identity.

So difficult.

Let's try giving ourselves permission

to blur the familiar image.
Zap the mirror, turn the surface wavy
like a movie flashback.

Impossible. We are who we've been, what we've done.
Well, yes, but let's look harder. There's more too.
Drag the mind down, down below memory even.
Rescue the lost dreams, barely visible, lingering
in a dark corner.

That's a distant image, harder to see, keeps moving.
What's forgotten back there?
What's possible still?
What's worth our last, unrequired,
personally heartfelt effort?

No, not a legacy, not even a final heroic act (though
either might result).

What we're looking for's more like an utterly
uncalled-for cry into the wind.
A longing passed over, extraordinary only in
its origins, its passing through so clearly from the soul,
then carried away unnoticed like any ordinary breath.

So that passed-over longing's not really ordinary,
far from it. Some central part of us may have been

stuffed down in all the get-ahead rush.

Time now to choose carefully from that core.
    Re-mind.
    Re-member.
    Re-invest.
What part of ourselves has been left behind?
To make room in our guts, we'll have to digest
the nearly indigestible.
Swallow hard ...
We'll never get to do everything we want to do,
be everything we want to be.
Not even if we only try to finish
what we've already begun.
Let that in.
No. Not enough time left.
Well, maybe ... if we live to be very, very old ...
No, not even then. Because doing anything,
like learning,
creates a whole new list of possibilities.
So, shall we quit? Lie down? Have we done enough?
No, never.

So what now? A bunch of years still left;
how do I want to spend them?
    Hold it!
    Wait a minute.

Go slow.
There's an *outside answer* and an *inside answer*.

What do we mean by *an outside answer?*

The *outside* ... who we've appeared to be,
what we've done, may create a blinding flash
in front of our inner eye, distort our true
present vision like an after-image remaining too long.

Seeing through or around that familiar image
may be almost impossible. After all, it took all these
years to create. We've become used to looking at it,
believing it. We forget it's also in our way.
Old expectations intrude, push their way into
our musings, take up all the space.

So set that outside stuff aside—the accomplishments,
the titles, the status, the job descriptions.
(The skills remain; they're part of us.)
Now attend to the inside. That's the right priority
for this life phase.
Check in ... and in ... and in ...
on what remains.

Another life-segment to live. Scraped together
out of all the leavings of our past.

Another life-part of however-many-years
yet to enjoy.

We get to create this one with new colors—only dimly
glimpsed perhaps, but sensed, intuited.
A new chance for the next twenty minutes or thirty
years—our poorer vision clarifying the view into
the darker corners we've ignored, rushed past,
or shoveled full of pretense.

Another inner argument erupts.

"What's in there? Is there time to look?"

"There'll never be enough time."

"So it's urgent, isn't it? Last call for this round."

"Not yet, surely."

"Oh yeah? Then when?"

"What? Who me?" (Still resisting?) "When? What am I
supposed to do? Can't I just let the years take me along?
I'm tired. My head hurts. We'll talk more later."

"No, now."

"But how shall I think about this?"

"How about a list of *wants* and *don't-wants*?"

"Oh no, not a list! There are hundreds of them scattered
in my wake like feathers. Lists ... years full of lists,
my life-stuffing falling behind me, crossed out,
discarded, lost. Lists. To do. To remember.
To finish. To call. To answer.
Lists marking my way to the next accomplishment.
Trailing after me, blown into yesterday's leavings.
No, please, not another list!"

"Well then, try a picture. A visual image in your mind.
No need for paper. Just imagine you've passed through
that door, like the people who've died and come back.
The *tunnel of light*, you know. And then you decide
you need some more time here, and return."

"When you open your eyes, what do you first wish for?
    "What do you want to see?
    "What hunger isn't satisfied?
    "Nothing? Confusion, you say?"

Suggestion: see under several very big headings,
universal, ageless
    Beauty

Beauty
Truth
Goodness
Wonder
Connection
Courage

Let's give it a concentrated try. Even if our senses are somewhat dimmer, our attention span's much better than when we were five or even thirty-five.

EGIN WITH *BEAUTY*

An artist friend of mine died recently, leaving
an immense, unfillable hole in my life. Since we
lived on opposite sides of the country these last
years, I pretend she's still in Boston, only not home
to receive my phone call.

It's not only a pretense. She's part of every
moment I'm aware of the beauty in my everyday
surroundings. More than any other person
she taught me to be on the lookout, to prowl
around the ordinary, rescuing the sacred from
the mundane. Nothing escaped her. When she was
by my side, I sprouted six pairs of eyes and a cat's
hearing. "There's beauty everywhere," she said,
"but you have to be awake. Don't even blink;
you might miss something."

Who'd say no to *Beauty*? Bathing our (slightly
less blazing) senses, filling the tub with oils
and sweet scents, letting our sight and hearing wander
over the world's wonder?

Okay. *Beauty* where?

Starting with *Nature*—but not just flying past

out car windows, hidden by a cloud bank under
the plane's belly.

Nature: viewed at leisure.

In detail:
animals, trees, flowers, mountains, oceans
and skies, minute creatures going about their business.
Notice what's visible, even without a microscope,
in one-square-foot of ground.
(But with a magnifying glass—wow!)

Ponder the shapes of dustballs, cobwebs,
old orange peels,
dried leaves.

Look around.

Catch *People-Beauty*, click!
Faces: young and old, expressions in repose, in action,
caught in a second like a camera, trapped in the eye,
enhancing, challenging outworn apprehensions,
demanding another opinion on what's lovely, ugly,
worth another look.

Get the children. Fast forward.
Rampantly fresh, hopeful, even if trampled. Not yet

lost. Unfrozen for awhile, the possible still pending.
Muscles and spirit mobile. Their youth attracts our age
like magnets, pulling us into tomorrows they'll see
and hear and touch for us, demanding from us one last
energetic thrust upward in their name.

Study the *Body-Beautiful*. Any body. Mine, yours, theirs.
Arms, legs, and hips in motion, leaping, stretched, and
curled in our stead.

Our daily exercise to stay in shape slams us
against our age limits. But jumping and diving
with the Olympiads, we can stay *behind*
our eyes and be *limitless* ...

Our full-hearted pleasure's possible if we finally admit
that nobody's checking us out anymore.
And it's too late to run the fastest mile.

Yes, it's obvious now ... *We'll never have that perfect body.*
Which, once admitted, leaves us freed up to look again.
Body: a miraculous construction—
part of this world's beauty.
Body: an intricate, sublimely synchronized,
tick-tocking symphony of moving parts.

Look! His muscles draw an unexpected shape against

the sun, curving the air. Her perfect form focuses
our eyes on one small silhouette of light between
a fingertip

and ball, a thigh and wooden bar, ribcage and wire,
toe and chalkline.
More than vicarious delight.
With no preconditions for wonderment.
We're *inside*, looking out ...
We get to set aside the magazines, movies,
sight-washing media. Appreciate the surfaces,
skin textures, wrinkles, endless varieties of line
and color.

We can re-form, re-vitalize our vision, more precious
as it fades.

We can visit the zoo or walk in the woods. Watch
nature programs. See animals, insects, fish and birds
as if they're new on the planet. Take nothing
for granted.

We can join the babies, studying a primal world.
In this last nick of time, learn to appreciate what is,
rather than what's missing.

Yes, we have a lot missing these days in comparison

to the ads. But we're not helpless yet to change our
way of seeing.

Sound-Beauty. (Even through age-dulled hearing.)
Listen.
Hear music everywhere. If we're lucky, the formal kind,
complete with saxophones and clarinets.
Turn up the volume if necessary. Radios are cheap.
Sing along. Who cares if the voice cracks?
That humming in the head and throat tingles
the nerve endings.

Still alive. Yes.
Besides, the deep breathing's good for the lungs.
Pass the song around. Smile. We're on *Candid Camera.*
Let the audience laugh.

Did I always want to play the piano, the harp,
the violin? So it'll take ten years to learn it, and I'll never
be a star. I still might have ten or more years to enjoy
my autumnal virtuosity. Maybe even form a band,
a chamber group, a trio, with my friends.
Stop shaking your head. This too is possible.

And other music—the subtler kind, in voices,
familiar and new:
          baby-gurgles,

throaty whispers in the night,
screams of delight,
giggles, panic, and pleas
for understanding, help, pardon

Music in ordinary sounds.
Grinding machinery on the road, in kitchens,
cleaners, offices.
Tap water running into the sink.
The cat lapping up milk; the sleeping dog
whimpering and woofing in its dream.
The soft singing of nature—wind, birds, streams
and rivers, frogs, crickets.
Generic snaps, rustles, clicks.

And words spoken. Even uncalled for.
There's time now, not so threatening to hear another
idea, a different notion, an off-the-wall comment
from a kid.

Hey, you!
A spontaneous whoop on a street corner
could open a new corridor in our neatly
arranged directional system.

Welcome the noise as stimulant rather than intrusion.
Recharge our batteries for free while we still live here.

Can all this be called *Beauty*?
Perhaps. Not always, but surprisingly often.

Noisy youngsters in every era know something.
We can be archetypal grandparents—listening,
hearing, seeing beauty, rather than clucking away
their ungracious remarks.

Take a nap if it gets too bad.

And Still More Beauty

How about touching? Lots of squeezes and hugs.
Let the nerve ends linger a little longer if need be.
A little more time, perhaps. Fortunate there's a bit
more available these days.

(We had to be quick when we were younger—cram
the pleasures in when the kids were asleep or the boss
was away. The young blood roared, charged into
action at a second's notice.)

Loitering now allowable. Coffee smells wafting
into the bedroom don't hurtle us out of bed. Time for
skin tracing, sweet talk, long pauses.
Even lying there alone, the sheets falling lightly on
the thin skin, we simmer in familiar juices.

Memories tremble on waking edge, make us smile.
Or cry for long-ago love. "Better to have lost than
never won." Oh yes, much better.

The old woman's hands slide back and forth,
back and forth, over the satin robe, the wooden
chair arm.

He walks barefoot in the garden when he's watering.
Grass-prickles and fresh mud tickle his toes and arches.

She cups the flowers gently in her palm, letting
their fragility travel down her arm, trigger her
mind-holdings into forgotten lines of poetry,
the softness of newly washed baby blankets.

And we still have our noses:
smell the mint in the tabouli, sweet basil and garlic
in the pesto, tarragon in the salad. Use twice as
much as we used to when our taste was more
delicately tickled.

(Thank the Nose God for the odors that don't
reach us anymore.)
Instead: crush bay leaves, plant jasmine by the front
door. Set narcissus in bowls. Toss spices into
boiling water when company's coming. (Or we're

trying to sell the house.)
Bury our faces in roses and gardenias, or even
geraniums and oleanders.
Sniff harder if need be.

And movement—slower perhaps (how come all these
moving parts get creaky?)

We boast of some major exceptions: our marathon
runners, septuagenarian athletes. Tennis, anyone?
Hikers and walkers out there, lots of them. And
dancers? Over-sixty champions abound.
Not I, you say? Well, nearly everybody moves.
Step, sway and turn, if the legs and arms are up to it.
Go on! Nobody's looking. Rhythm and beat
are blessings free for the taking.
Shake out the back and belly. Even a finger, a toe
tapping will allow the two-four, three-four punch
to enter the blood and sinews.
Feels good. Yes.

What more for *Beauty*?
Painting and art. No need to rush in and out of old
public buildings without looking up and noticing
the doorways, the walls, the facades. Enjoy gazing.
Better yet, create our own. Call it art. Not too late.
Play with clay. Sew, weave, knot, carve, hammer,

knit, weld, crochet. Make presents for everyone.
(Never ask if they use them.)

Draw pictures.
Just for the sake of seeing more vividly.

Sit on a comfortable seat in a gallery and stare
at a picture for fifteen minutes, minimum.
Trace patterns in the dirt, make sandcastles,
arrange flowers.

And yes, of course, grow things, if there's a piece
of ground or even a container, a window box. Just
for the pleasure of following the growing cycle,
seeing the first bit of green push through the soil.
If we can produce real food, so much the better.

Well, enough of *Beauty*?
No, never enough. Everywhere and all the time.
Even shadows on walls create mosaics.

(A near-blind, paralyzed, old lady laughingly
described rainbows of colors all around our heads.
She saw them.)

Hang a mobile, put a daisy in a vase, a fern in the
corner. Throw a colored cushion on the old couch.

Blow up balloons. Hang them with paper streamers
where the breeze catches them.

The point is not to close our eyes and ears before
they're closed for us. While we have them, celebrate
their possibilities.

Sense-loaded. Drunk with delight. And mindless,
or is it mind-full?

Bringing us to another subject: *mind*.
I'd so hoped ... one day I'd know *The Truth*.
(Note the capitals.)
I've given up on that. Oh well ... so, *I'll never know
all the answers*.

WHAT OF *TRUTH?*

Old Jerome, round, bald and bespectacled, has been
behind the counter of his little jewelery shop
for forty years. He specializes in old jewelery
which he takes on consignment, cleans and
repairs, splitting the resale profit with the owners.

Actually, his store is a front.
The assorted characters coming and going are looking
for something other than family heirlooms.

Along with a few stray customers hoping for bargains,
there's always an assembly of aging philosophers
or would-be theologians, sipping coffee in paper cups
carried in from next door, arguing in soft voices,
settling the serious matters of the universe.

Somehow, Jerome has scraped by, managed
to support a wife, get his kids through college
using his clever hands, while never relinquishing
his passion for learning. Books and papers fill
every available counter, pile up on chairs.

Once I tripped over a bearded guru sitting
cross-legged in the corner mumbling
his mantra.

In his younger years Jerome wandered over Israel,
India, Tibet, China, searching, as he puts it, for
Ultimate Truth. Finally, he spent months alone,
writing out his personal creed according to which
he then proceeded to live out his years.

As for *Truth*, he realized it was really the search
he loved, that, like Rilke, he hoped the questions
might lead one day into the answers. But if not,
the journey was never dull.

The Truth becomes more elusive (illusive)
all the time.

Our minds bang open and shut on worn hinges,
so many years of arriving at closure, only to fly
open again. So, who knows?

Yes? Well. Some of us have a few absolutes lying
around. They somehow survived the various and
assorted revolutions—sexual, economic, technological,
philosophical, theological. Whatever these kinds of
truths are, it's probably best at this stage
not to insist on proving them to anybody.
Simply live them out if they work for us.

Even more important: maintain our reverence

for our truths whatever they may be.
Time to think now ... eyes closed or staring into space.
Time to locate the meaning beneath the beliefs.
Time to turn that meaning into prayer.
Use our beliefs for strength.
Draw on those beliefs for endurance, love, compassion.
Extend their firmness into the despair of others
less anchored, more buffeted by fate and circumstance.

No, not with sermons.
Let's just stand silent with ourselves unless we're
asked, our thoughts inquired upon or sought.
Keep our own faith, whatever it may be, however
arrived at.
It can't be handed over, anyhow.

The very fact of believing in something enough
to hope—yes, that's the gift we have to give.
Endurance. Fortitude. Faith. The willingness
to learn. And more ...

Why not include all gifts of the mind under *Truth*?
Expand the label. Make it more fun.
We can play with thought, toss ideas around,
quietly, in puzzled or amused silence.
(Solitary confinement appears suddenly desirable,
at least the *no interruptions* part.)

Mind-wrestling, mental handsprings
to inward applause.

Or dream-gazing into unexplored regions,
tagging a new notion and running with it,
having caught just a glimpse
of a miracle. Unable to follow yet, but promising
to return at the very next meditative moment.

Or thought-play with others. *Thinking aloud.*
Conversation. Discussion. Duets or chorus.
Diagrams created in thin air out of breath, voice,
and mind.

Insight-exchange: can turn a head inside out, create
laughter, fright, tears, anger, affection, disdain,
unexpected paralysis.

That's the glory of, that's the story of words!
Yes, words. Sling them, float them, bounce them
back and forth, get ensnarled, entangled, alienated,
supported, inspired. Or bored, sometimes.
All for free.

Just words, only words, strung together with
or without forethought. Words between persons.
Building bridges, barriers, embraces, wars, walls,

elevators, tunnels, and deep, bottomless pits.

Handle with care.
A four-letter word for intercourse
is *talk*.

Or words strung together in lines, written down
to insure survival, guard against dissolution.
On paper, stone, pavement, shouting out
in bathrooms and subways, *I was here!*

Or more formally: words printed by certain
knowing persons on heavy paper, bound together
between sturdy covers to last.

Someone important, with excellent taste
and impeccable credentials (and probably power
or money), has decided to save these particular
thoughts for our children's children's children.

Bringing us to:
books!
Railways of print to take us anywhere, shelf upon
shelf, ladders to summit views, enchantment.

Books! (This library smell makes me feel starving,
insatiable.)

Words again. But oh, what words! Sentences,
paragraphs, marching along together, margins
aligned. Or standing singly with squeaky clean
exclamation points strategically placed,
commanding attention.

Words: lined up neatly, eternally, for the mind's
inspection, review, reflection, imitation, delight.
Written words. Carrying us across boundaries
we can only cross if no one can listen in, spy, or tell.

Onward!

Into exotic countries where, if we were caught,
we'd be found wanting.
    "Not poetic enough!"
    "Not well enough educated."
    "Not experienced enough!"
    "Lacking in philosophical insight!"

The books in our hands don't care who we are,
sitting here
under the lamp, greedily gobbling up their print,
turning pages fast as we can go.
(If we can't see very well, actors with gorgeous voices
read to us on tape. Just press a button.)
The books don't laugh or throw us off the train.

Don't tell us that we're too fat, too old, too ignorant, too awkward, too fearful for this heady, amorous, inspiring, thrill-filled adventure. We can go anyhow.

Yipee!

Thank you for glorious transport: Emily, Dylan, Ezra, T.S., e.e., Jane, William and Walt, Henry, Albert, Gabriel, Adrienne, Virginia, Doris, Collette, Charlotte, Annie and James, all four Evangelists.

Thank you, thinkers, philosophers, the millions
of word-wizards who hang around permanently
in my head, creating non-stop magic.
And since we know now that *we'll never read
all the books that we yearn to read ...*
We better enjoy what we can.
Make way for endless fascination.
The *Truth-search* never ends. Does it?

With our last breath will we say with Gertrude,
"What is the question?" Wish we'd wagered with Pascal?

Will we refuse to go "gentle into that good night,"
because we've still so much to learn?

Will we be newly energized by startling information

beamed daily from the Hubble Telescope?

Will we just be getting started on Ariel and Will Durant's history series, waiting for a decade on our bookshelf?

Will we still be memorizing the British line of succession?

Will we still be trying to understand photosynthesis, define quarks, remember the final lines of *Four Quartets*?

Ruminating with Hegel, Aristotle, Kierkegaard?

Will we wish another hundred years to discover, investigate, categorize, mull-over, and digest?

Yes. Oh yes. Undeniably, yes.

Will we want to hang around for coming attractions?
Probably.

In our lonely three-in-the-morning darkness,
we find it poignantly impossible to believe ... *We'll never see the future.*
But Lord! What we've already seen!

Remember when the year 2000 was only in science fiction? Our grandchildren don't even hesitate over

the number. "Next century," they mutter casually.
Our list of wonders bores them. We recite them
to one another when they're not around, our thirst
for more increasing as we savor the possibilities
in store.

If humans can walk on the moon, is anybody else
out there? If wind and ocean produce energy,
is the source endless?

Are we programmed for self-destruction or eternal
life? Should we try to do everything we know
how to do?

Is it possible we'll know all the answers from some
other (ad)vantage point?

Awe-struck, we shake our heads, ponder
the imponderable,
fall silent.

BUT WE CAN WONDER

Yes, there's time for that. We wonder:
if we'll ever know what's next. Or if all wonder
ceases with our breath.

Yes, finally, we know enough to pause.
To stare in (dis)belief.
Shut out the celebration and the noise, the chatter
of the explanations.
Yes, this we know: to try, however briefly, just to
take it in.

Someone(s) with brains and hearts and hands like ours
have done these things, for better or for worse,
have made such miracles. They've stood on one
another's shoulders, to set our world on fire
    to make it visible in whole and part,
    to challenge every preconception that we hold,
    to push us, gape-mouthed, into wordless
    wonder.

This we can do: be thoughtful, grateful, hold to *hope*.
And, just because we've been here for awhile,
(we like to think of it as perspective), remind one another,
and anyone else who's interested, this may be
only the beginning.

As the kids would say, "Awesome!"
We wonder if we matter.

Oh, we will leave our mark! Maybe *mine* will be
lost in *yours* and *ours*, but we will affect the future.
Yes. However we walk here today changes
the landscape for centuries or even forever
for our younger friends and theirs.

Will we growl and stamp around with heavy feet,
snuffing out dreams?
Or learn to step gently as our own bones lighten,
tread carefully on a fragile earth?
Can we put aside our jealousies, the gnawing awareness
we're somewhat peripheral to future speculations?
Can we become benign, shoved to the sidelines?
Can we cheer our inheritors on whole-heartedly?
Too much to ask?
Oh well ...

It's undoubtedly true that ... *We'll never be as good
as we always meant to be. So ...*

How About *GOODNESS*?

We'd better make way for a new version
of *Goodness*.

Yes, we notice *Goodness*, like *Truth*, changing form
a lot over the years.

The dark and the light switch places.
Dad and Mom line up on the scale differently
than they used to. Also the kids.
To say nothing of assorted friends, relatives,
people in the news.
And, of course, ourselves.
Success, as it turns out, often has
an underside.
Virtue remains suspect.
Heroes and villains switch masks
when we're not looking.
Saviors turn into jailers.
And vice versa.

Hard to judge and make the judgment stick
over time. Better not to generalize, moralize,
make rigid rules
that guarantee surprising overturns
and contradictions in the next mail.

Although, as with *Truth*, a few absolutes
can offer some relief.
Like Nyquil, for a good night's rest.

Well, by the time we're this age,
have we pretty much decided on our moral boundaries?
This far, but no farther. For ourselves. For others.
Probably. It's just too uncomfortable otherwise.
What's *Goodness* got to do with this final life
segment anyway? Is it even worth discussing?
"For goodness' sake, yes!" we say. And some of us add,
"For heaven's sake," as well.

An ordinary conversation about *Goodness*:
"What do I think about *Goodness*?" my friend says,
as he stands in the kitchen pulling leaves off a stem
of tarragon. (The chicken in the pan waits patiently
to hear.) "My friends are good."

"What's that mean?" persisting.

"Oh, I believe they're honest. Or try to be.
Do what they say they'll do. Or tell me if they can't.
They won't desert in rough times. I can't think about
Goodness except attached to someone I care about."

"Not any rules," his wife interrupts from the sink.

"As sure as you make one, someone you think
is good will break it, and you'll have to change
your definition."

"Or your friend," he responds. "Or maybe just insert
a question mark after his name where there used
to be a period."

"Compassion," she adds. "A capacity for empathy.
A willingness to forgive. Loyalty, not the slavish kind,
but a protective impulse toward the loved one.
And kindness, just the down-home welcome to another
of earth's wanderers, a warm fire and a chair."

Another voice speaks up for generosity, largeness
of spirit. The clichés tumble out: dependability,
integrity, humility, perspective.
There in the kitchen, fixing dinner, we find ourselves
agreeing easily. And wonder what some other group
would say. And why it matters, anyhow.
But it does. Goodness matters.
Our last chance to *right the wrongs*,
if we can decipher them.
To be a *Worthy Person*. (Big, important words,
a royal title.)

Yes, *Goodness* matters. To gather up some scattered seeds

of pain, wind up dishonest yarns, blow clean
air through the pollution of our arrogances
and hypocrisies.
If we can't go back to fix things in flesh and blood,
we can in spirit bind the wounds,
make the amends, forgive ourselves
and everybody else.

It's not too late. Yet.
Carry on—have a heart. Put it in the voice
and on the face.
Please. Thank you.
You're welcome.
I'm sorry.
I forgive myself.
I forgive you.
You can do it!
I can do it.
I love you.
Take care.
See you tomorrow.

Say them all because ... *We know now we'll never have
enough time with those we love.*
Which brings us to ...

CONNECTIONS

Missy, at 90, has been widowed eight years.
Over her birthday lunch she tells me stories of her
57-year marriage. I can see she enjoys the telling.
The memories bring her husband out of memory
darkness into present daylight.

If she speaks of him aloud and of their life together,
she can share the presence she usually carries alone
in her heart, in the back of her mind.

My favorite story is one she has told many times.
She savors the telling. It seems that her great aunt
stole a white rose from Missy's wedding bouquet,
rooted it, and planted it in a pot. When the bride
and groom moved into their first home, she presented
it to them as a house-warming gift.

For their fiftieth wedding anniversary party,
her husband picked a rose from the bush to wear
in his lapel. Missy, the tears standing in her clear
blue eyes, tells me, "It's hard to believe, but you know
that bush died the same year he did."

I notice as I grow older the increasing simultaneity
of love and pain. I had glimpses of this when I was

younger, but now it's inescapable. My husband puts his arms around me, and I want to become absolutely absorbed into him. In the very same second, I want to push him away, get busy with something else. I want to smile and laugh with pleasure and I want to explode into tears.

This dance of intimacy isn't new,
but it's more poignant,
more pervasive, more intrusive these days.
On one level, my seemingly contradictory impulses make perfect sense. How can I bear to let myself feel his closeness, depend on his presence, knowing someday we will part? This was always true.
Only now *someday* is moving closer and closer with every tick of the clock.

We'll never really be ready to leave our loved ones behind (or to be left).
The more reason to relish the moments, the deeper, well–constructed *connections*.

Yes, more dear than ever.

Over lunch, a friend says, "Let's keep current."
I'm grateful for the reminder.
Let's remember to say the taken–for–granteds.

When her husband thought
he was having a heart attack,
his (in)sight was restored, like the blind man
in the Bible.

Now they play together more.
Dinner with the family these days rends the heart.
"My, how you've grown." Got to stop saying that
every time we see the kids.

We remember when their Mom's front teeth
were missing
and her knees perpetually bandaged.
She smiles back at us now, tiny wrinkles forming
around her eyes.
Arrivings and departings aren't so casual anymore.
"See you later." Let us pray.

So everybody's just discovered bonding.
How about unbonding?
There's lots of that these late-life days.
They move away or die, leaving a large unfillable hole.
It hurts to think about them.
But we do.

The ache says "No," and then we comfort ourselves,
"It's only for awhile." And maybe that's true, but

there's no guarantee in this life, or whatever's next.

We hurt from stretching across lands, through time, into other worlds. Our grip tightens, loosens, gives way. And we grab on again. One moment's comfort in a photograph, a tape recording, a home video.

"Oh, look, there he is!" And then the emptiness again.

"She lives on the East Coast, you know, with her husband and children."

"He died four years ago. Very sudden."

"She had a stroke. She'll never be the same."

Light candles, say *Kaddish*, sing *Requiem*, have a wake, keep a vigil, walk in procession, beat the drum slowly.

Unbonding? No such thing.
The connections remain.
The real ones do. And why not? This link's not formed for decay, earthy material like stone or rock.
Muscle and sinew weaken.But
    memory
    soul–meeting

heart-touching
These outweather them all.

"Not of this world," we whisper, not quite sure what
we mean, except a word, a voice, a view,
a certain laugh, a joke, an unexpected touch
brings everything awake again.
What, still attached?

Oh yes. Some bonds endure. We know which ones
by the time we're this age.
It's harder to fool us with false promises. (And when
we fall for sham, it's usually quite temporary.)

Of course, if we disconnect—physically, mentally,
emotionally—(Who wants to think about it?)
we only hope someone we love stays on the line.
        Holds on.
        Ignores the buzz.
        Calls back if we hang up on them.

So what's it worth, all this *connection*?
These bonds that only end up causing pain?
End up?
What's this about an *End*?

Yes, that's the tough part, isn't it?

Love, laughter, life: it ends.
Abruptly, even if expected.

Before. Now. After … all move continuously:
circling, overlapping, familiar, surprising.
We've learned to leap, skip, run, but not … stop.
The End's what we don't know how to do yet.

The End just sits out there watching, the big
timekeeper, becoming more and more engorged
on our precious moments.

The End … looming, mind-deadening. Presence
of our later days.

So if it has so much power anyhow, why not
march right up to it and take a closer look?

Whither goest thou, *Big E*?
"Enlivening, aren't I?" it roars back.
The *Big E* in our heads reminds:
look for the enduring, the eternal.
Live it up to the last experience.
The *Big E* dares us each and every day.

It's such a mystery, this *End*. Who really believes
it will happen to him? To her? Do you?

Maybe that's a clue.

They told us when we were little about devils
and stern judges out there waiting, tearing us
away from our loyal band of admirers, protectors,
useful friends, and lovers. We'd better get ready
to prove ourselves.

Oh, yeah, sure. We thought we'd have it all
figured out by now.
Death comprehended perfectly, blueprint for a future
life. Cross over confidently.

Well, we still rather like the idea of certainty.
But, let's face it, there's only this moment
for sure (and the time-and-matter guys
even wonder about *that*.)

Well, all right. On to *The End*. Challenge the *stop*
with *start*.
If we have faith in a continuing life, let's keep it alive.

Make our own definition of *The End*, the one that
lingers in us anyhow—whatever the cynical judges
have to say.
How about *happily ever after*?
There's an old one, well used, relied on

for thousands of years. Why not pick that?
Happily ever after. The End.

So childlike …
Yes. Wise old children that we are, we realize our
fears exactly match our vision of *The End*.
So we may as well make it a happy one.
Stand close, hold hands, together to *The End*.

Living to The End

So now if we can concentrate, unhampered,
on the here and now, who or what would we like
on the other end of our string?
Possibilities boggle the mind:
in addition to whoever's around to love in our past
or present, there's still coming attachments in store
for some who are daring. (One woman I know fell
madly in love in her nineties.)

For those who aren't even looking, perhaps some
quiet, unsolicited adventures are in store, some we'll
only recognize when they sneak up on us and give
the secret handshake.

The most important thing is to attach.
That's where the juices are.

Without some yeasty attachments we go flat,
fail to rise.

A new connection …
to an idea, a cause, an experience,
most especially a person, transforms inert cells
into inebriating fluids, stirs up a mess
of new combinations
to deal with.

Connection: internal combustion
to get the old motor running. A little garlic,
a bit of lemon, some horseradish (perhaps)
thrown into a bland mix.

"When I see your face across the room, I smile inside."

"I could sit and watch this baby all day."

"Yesterday I marched in my first peace demonstration."

"Just the sound of your voice on the phone
lifts my spirits."

A friend in her eighties whose *work* is gardening
and visiting the elderly announced at breakfast
that she just couldn't wait to begin her day.

A Midwest newspaper pictures a smiling grandfather
in his seventies waving from an open cockpit.
His grandson-instructor, seated behind him, checks
the instrument panel.

Late into the night, an old lady, crooning softly,
sits rocking an AIDS baby.

The retired carpenter curls arthritic fingers
around the wrench in the boy's hand: "This way;
you're doing fine."

A big paradox (just to complicate matters):
we can only dare to be attached when we're unattached.
Lots of years and the losses that come with them
have taught us that.
Need to hold our end of the string lightly—
for comfort, affection, concern—all those good things.
And more. But ready to let go.
Ready? Come on! Who's ever really *ready* to let go?
A few saints, maybe, or so they tell us. Even Jesus
complained a bit.

Nevertheless, there aren't any great alternatives.
Winding the string tightly, pulling it in, feels safe
sometimes. But then, where's the *Other*?
All gagged and bound, molded to my already

suffocating self. Who's to love? What's to save?
Where's the lover? Neither of us needs this.
And the separating still happens.
Only it rips us up a lot more.

Forced to learn all this stuff in our later life.
For the first time or the thousandth, over and over.
Separating happens.
Love and let go.

l can't!
Well, we'll have to practice.
Try a loose hold instead of just running away scared
and empty-handed.
We'll have to practice:
     letting the kite fly higher and higher
     riding the waves
     going easy in the saddle
     bouncing the ball back lightly
     breathing out slowly

We'll have to get proficient at staying in (gentle)
touch with the moment.
Holding the hand held out to us
Offering our own with no stickiness in the palm.

So many ways to connect if we don't need a lot

of trophies. Or to know how it all turns out.
We've got the stuff.
All these years of mistakes, makeovers,
trials and errors.
Some shopworn skills,
lots of taken-for-granted-know-how.
And probably more time to concentrate
than ever before.

We Can Give

Somebody out there can use what we know.
The newspapers, and television, tell us every day,
call out to us.
Kids' eyes look back, desperate moms, discouraged
workers, strung-out guys giving up on themselves.
Plenty to do. No problem there.

We can be useful.
Hard to let that in.
Hard to move.
Hard to begin.
We think all the helping years are behind us.

"Done enough. Tried hard enough."

"Let the young ones do it now."

Fair enough. But then, no bellyaching about being disconnected, overlooked, left out. Okay?

We can continue to do our bit, even though …
We'll never affect our world as much as we'd hoped.
But do we have any *power* left?

That's a big word these days. (Yes, the usual kind is still purchased. Money still matters. Whether we like it or not. Care, comfort, medicine, bed, board— all for sale. Not cheap. Some can buy. Some cannot.)

Are we pulling out? Staying in? Or are we set aside?

Some of us get to choose. And others just get pushed. Yeah, that's still the way it is.

Courage

There are lots of us around these days.
With more coming every year. A big bunch of us
scaring the youngsters witless with our numbers.
Imagine elders with clout!

So who thinks we'll be wise and generous? Speak up!
The answer's building to a huge crescendo out there.
Only it's still hard to hear.
And when we do hear who we've become as a group,
will we be proud of ourselves?
Shall we remain connected enough to each other,
to this world, to get involved? To be of use?

"Oh, no! I've done all that," you protest.
"This time of my life is just for me."

Don't panic. It can be different this time.
Less pressure from outside and in,
more natural timing. A little here, a little there.
A bit of smoothing, rubbing,
hugging, listening, scribbling, answering, pasting,
or stuffing. A smile, a hug, a word, a conversation.

Not so quick as we once were, maybe. Muscles
complain sooner. But the spirit holds, doesn't collapse

in the push and shove, has lasted through longer
and tougher struggles.

Our capacity for *not noticing* the insults to our
superior selves has grown.
We can work now for the sake of the doing.
We're pretty good at cleaning up the debris
    picking through the leftovers
    saving the scraps
    bolstering a tiny corner of the big tent
Out of the spotlight; no applause necessary.

Each of us can be one among many.
    Not a Messiah.
    Not Dorothy Day, Mother Theresa,
    Andrei Sakharov, Martin Luther King,
    Nelson Mandela, Eleanor Roosevelt.
    Not saint, martyr, leader, visionary.
    Not scholar, explorer, famous artist, writer, poet,
    performer, earth-changer, or tide-turner.
Just one among many. And we'll exit one day, while
some few cry, and most don't know the difference.

Who cares if we try? You. And I. And we. Just because
we're here now. And it's our circus while we're still
in the ring. No curtain calls till the show ends. And
who'll care then if nobody applauds?

So what if ... *We'll never be stars?*
We're a great bunch of *has-beens*
insisting on being here now.

Did we really hope to be stars one day?
Or is that just everybody's secret, vaguely
amorphous dream, the normal narcissism that
comes with having a separate skin and soul
of one's very own?

Did it feel the same to Leonard Bernstein or
Judy Garland to die alone as it will to me or you?
Does being famous make it harder, or easier?
The audience doesn't get to come. The clapping
and shouting grow still. Is the new silence welcome
and friendly?

For most ordinary folk solitude and silence creep in
along with the years. It's our call whether they close
us in, or open us up, are hostile or friendly.

One lady memorized Shakespeare for years so she'd
always have good company. When she went blind
and deaf in her eighties she shouted out the lines.
What's in our storehouse for the snowed-in days
ahead? Good eats for the mind and spirit have to be
gathered while we still have the energy.

Memories feed us too, if they're mulled over
lovingly, freely sprinkled
    with forgiveness
    time-ripened
    carefully selected for lasting flavor
Just throw out the rest.

Solitude slows us down inside to match the outside.
Stretches out and flattens the speeding days so they
can be appreciated.
Steadying a microscope takes very still hands.
Rushing won't do for the deeper inspection
these moments warrant. Need to study the details
when time's so precious.

Even if *ripeness is all* we still have to decide which fruit,
and when to pick.
Staring out of windows, sitting by water,
contemplating mountains, leaning into ancient
trees, feeling sun, wind, rain and soil.
Nothing new here but the pace.
We're out of time—we can take as long as we please.

So more and more appears within.
While aging bodies slowly shrivel and shrink,
the lighter-than-air within us (some call soul) inflates,
billows, and flies.

We travel unseen skies, and scurry home each time,
a little less attached to our earthy containment.
And, simultaneously, a little more in love with the
incredible beauty of the dust we're made of.

"Let me grow lovely growing old," the poet said.
"So many fine things do. Laces and ivory and gold,
and silks need not be new."

And another: "Let all go, then comes love."

Thanks to the high school teacher who made us
memorize those words against our youthful will.
Now we get to take them out of our back pocket
and (finally) understand them.

BEAUTY, TRUTH, GOODNESS, WONDER, CONNECTION, COURAGE

So, floating with the current, we grow old.
Bathing in poignant paradoxes,
Relishing the sweet-sad pleasures of a sunset swim,
muscles engaged and taut.
Yet, inadvertently, we dream of night,
of sinking slowly, gracefully, from this world's sight.
(A little later, perhaps. Under cover of darkness.)
Each stroke demands another letting go:
keep this and this awhile, for ballast.
But, look, this other has to go.
Yes, and this.
Oh no!
Yes, now, deep-six it.
What, never again?
No, never.
Soul-exercise—this decision-making.
We grow daily, as we die.

 **Elders Academy Press**

"What if we couldn't wait to be old, like a child can't wait to be an adult?"
—Nader R. Shabahangi, Ph.D.

As Elizabeth Bugental points out it is a pretty good bet that our old age will last at least as long as our adolescence. While most of us didn't plan out our life path during adolescence, if we are lucky we might have an opportunity to do so in old age. The question is do we have the courage to examine our fears, desires and motives and determine how we would like to live the last decades of our life.

Through partnership with writers, Elders Academy Press seeks to encourage us to approach the process of aging with consciousness and to direct our thinking toward the possibilities ahead.

The Press also seeks to help change cultural perceptions of the elderly and aging, which tend to largely focus on the negative. Why is it that young and middle-aged people often ignore the elderly or treat them with carelessness? How in our interactions with the elderly, can we remain open to what they have to offer us, not only because they have more life experience than we do, but also because they are entrusted in our care?

Finally, the Press seeks to help develop a vision of the Contemporary Elder—a person (or role) we are longing for—someone who through their life experiences and willingness to examine their life is able to embrace their own and our differences, hopes, successes, failures, and dreams.

Elders Academy Press was established in 2002 and is a program and publishing house of Pacific Institute and Pacific Institute Europe, both non-profit, public benefit organizations.

Based in San Francisco, Pacific Institute teaches new perspectives on aging in the field of gerontology and aims to reestablish the role of wisdom and eldership in our society. The Institute, founded in 1992, raises individual awareness, promotes social transformation, and helps advance, disseminate, and preserve knowledge in gerontological fields that focus on clinical, educational and human services purposes.

For more information about Pacific Institute, Pacific Institute Europe, and the publications of Elders Academy Press, please visit: *www.pacificinstitute.org; www.elders press.org* or *www.pacificinstitute-europe.org.*